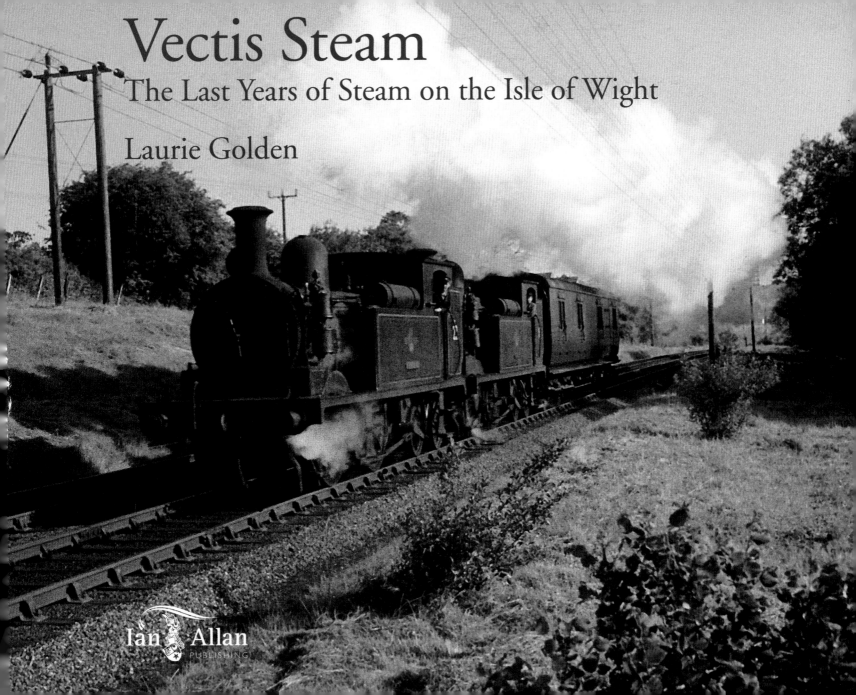

Vectis Steam
The Last Years of Steam on the Isle of Wight

Laurie Golden

Ian Allan PUBLISHING

Front cover: No 35 *Freshwater* climbing towards Smallbrook Junction on a Ventnor-line train during the summer of 1963.

Back cover: The single-line token for the Shanklin–Wroxall section is thrown to the signalman at Wroxall as No 30 *Shorwell* arrives with the 10.10 from Ryde to Ventnor in August 1963.

Previous page: One of two double-headed workings in 1965 was the 07.50 parcels train from Pier Head to Shanklin with the assisting engine detached at Sandown. In this view No 22 *Brading* pilots No 16 *Ventnor* near Smallbrook Junction. The vans would be stabled at Shanklin, and the locomotive used for further passenger working to Ryde.

First published 2011

ISBN 978 0 7110 3642 0

Published by Ian Allan Publishing

an imprint of Ian Allan Publishing Ltd, Hersham, Surrey, KT12 4RG
Printed in England by Ian Allan Printing Ltd, Hersham, Surrey, KT12 4RG

Code: 1105/B1

Distributed in the United States of America and Canada by BookMasters Distribution Services

Visit the Ian Allan Publishing website at www.ianallanpublishing.com

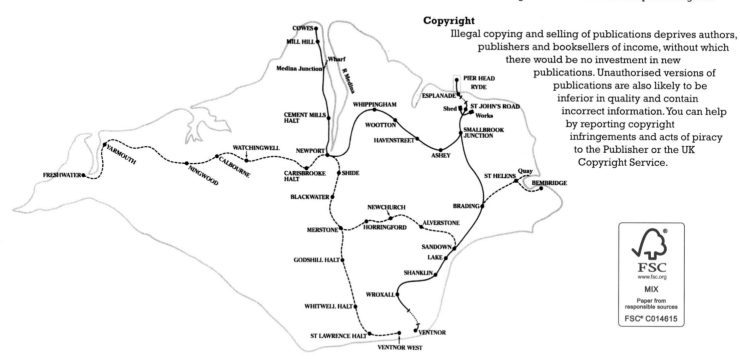

FSC
www.fsc.org
MIX
Paper from responsible sources
FSC® C014615

INTRODUCTION

Living in Surbiton, I found access to the Isle of Wight via the ferry from Portsmouth relatively straightforward, and its railways, representing a Victorian time-warp, were an obvious attraction. Numerous books and articles have already been written about the history of the island's railways, so in this volume I have concentrated on my own experiences and travels in the last four years of steam operation.

By 1963 the Newport–Freshwater, Newport–Sandown, Newport–Ventnor West and Brading–Bembridge lines had been long closed, leaving just those linking Ryde with Cowes and Ventnor. Steam traction was now represented by just one type, the 'O2' 0-4-4 tank engine (an Adams design of 1889), and for use on the island each of these locomotives had been modified with a Westinghouse brake and enlarged bunkers. Following closure of the Newport–Sandown line there remained no turning facilities on the island, and thereafter all the locomotives faced south. Coaching stock was primarily of LBSCR or SECR design, while many of the goods vehicles were of LBSCR or LSWR origin. The locomotive shed and works were located at St John's Road, a mile or so inland from the esplanade at Ryde.

At Ryde the railway ran right to the head of the pier, which gave direct access to the ferries to/from Portsmouth. The line to Ventnor ran in an essentially southerly direction from Ryde, relatively close to the east coast of the island, and served in particular the popular holiday resorts of Sandown and Shanklin. Diverging from the Ventnor line at Smallbrook Junction, the Cowes line ran in a westerly direction to Newport, the island's capital, before turning north to Cowes, on its northern tip. Newport and Cowes aside, this line served very sparsely populated areas and thus did not command anything like the levels of traffic enjoyed by the Ventnor route.

The Summer Saturday service on the island was of particular interest, due to the intensity of traffic on the Ventnor route. From about 09.00 to 17.00 the service on this line comprised four six-coach trains per hour in each direction, although only two per hour ran through to Ventnor itself, the other two terminating at Sandown or Shanklin. There was also one four-coach train per hour to Cowes. Apart from double-track sections between Ryde Pier Head and Smallbrook Junction (where the Cowes line diverged) and between Brading and Sandown the network was single-track, with passing loops at the major stations. With such an intensive service, any minor delay could snowball into serious disruption as the day progressed. During the week two trains per hour to Ventnor and one per hour to Cowes sufficed.

There was one further major attraction to the Summer Saturday service. There was insufficient siding space at Ryde to house during the week the extra coaching stock required for the Saturday, so some stock was stabled at Sandown and Shanklin. This meant that early on the Saturday morning locomotives had to be worked out to these locations to collect it. This was also convenient, as soon after nine o'clock holidaymakers were gathering at Sandown and Shanklin to begin their journeys home. To avoid the need for light-engine movements two early-morning trains southbound from Ryde Pier Head were double-headed, the first being the 07.40 passenger service to Ventnor, the second the 07.50 parcels to Shanklin. For those of us living on the mainland, photographing these trains was not easy. If one had accommodation on the island, the two trains ran at just the time that landladies wanted to serve breakfast, so I elected to travel from home in the small hours, catching the 06.00 ferry from Portsmouth, which arrived at Pier Head at 06.30. This connected with the

06.55 train to Ventnor, which could be used to travel to locations as far out as Shanklin. One way of catching this ferry was to take the last train from Surbiton to Waterloo and from there the 02.45 newspaper train to Portsmouth, which was steam-hauled via Basingstoke and Eastleigh (usually by a BR '76xxx'), but I soon found that I preferred to drive down from Surbiton to Portsmouth and leave the car there for the day.

By 1965, as the overworked 'O2s' began to wear out, the Motive Power Department was struggling to keep sufficient locomotives and coaching stock running to maintain the Summer Saturday service. As a result the closure was announced of all the island's railways, to take effect from 4 October 1965. However, public opinion — and the inability of road transport to cope with what was still a high volume of Saturday traffic from Sandown and Shanklin — forced a change of heart. As a compromise the line from Smallbrook Junction to Newport and Cowes was closed in February 1966, and the section of the southern line from Shanklin to Ventnor two months later. This meant that the locomotives and stock had to soldier on for a further summer, but by now the motive-power situation had become so critical that revised locomotive diagrams had to be issued late in May 1966 to cover the four-train-per-hour service to Sandown and Shanklin. Steam finally came to an end on 31 December 1966, and after winter closure the system reopened with former London Transport Underground stock running on third-rail electrified track from Pier Head to Shanklin.

To mark the end of steam two railtours were organised by the LCGB. The first ran on Sunday 3 October 1965 to mark what, at the time it was organised, was expected to be the last day of operation over the whole of the surviving system. The second ran on 31 December 1966, the end of steam working. As it transpired this was not the end of steam on the island. Today's Isle of Wight Steam Railway is located at Havenstreet, the midway point on the line from Smallbrook Junction to Newport, and runs services from a separate platform at Smallbrook Junction to Wooton, a couple of miles west of Havenstreet. Moreover, the society has preserved one of the 'O2s', *Calbourne*, and some of the original steam-era rolling stock.

Because I had a trackside pass for all the non-electrified lines on BR's Southern Region many of the photographs in this book are taken from lineside locations as well as stations. These photographs are arranged in geographical sequence in three sections, namely Ryde Pier Head–Smallbrook Junction, Smallbrook Junction–Ventnor and Smallbrook Junction–Cowes, followed by an end-of-steam finale. There is also an appendix, complete with diagram, plotting the pathways and passing-places (taken from the 1963 working timetable) over a one-hour cycle on a Saturday at the height of the summer service, which clearly demonstrates the importance of maintaining point-to-point times in adhering to the published schedule.

I hope you enjoy reading this book as much as I have enjoyed compiling it.

Laurie Golden
Cowbridge
January 2011

RYDE PIERHEAD–SMALLBROOK JUNCTION

Ryde Pier Head stands well out into the Solent, and the trains run right to the end. The signalbox which controlled all the movements down the pier is prominent in this August 1966 view, recorded around midday as a Shanklin-line train is departs.

Above: Pier Head station comprised four tracks around two island platforms. Here No 22 *Brading* (by now minus nameplates) is leaving for Sandown on an early-evening departure in August 1966.

Right: A busy period at Pier Head in 1964. From left to right, No 14 *Fishbourne* waits on an empty-stock train, No 35 *Freshwater* has been released from an earlier train and is waiting to back onto the next arrival, No 27 *Merstone* is on a train for Cowes, and No 28 *Ashey* is about to depart for Ventnor.

Above: As late as 1965 the intensive Summer Saturday service required strict punctuality to avoid accumulating delays, and a mishap on the pier certainly threw the system into disarray. In this late-afternoon scene No 22 *Brading* has become derailed close to the Pier Head station, and No 28 *Ashey* is in attendance with the breakdown crew. Meanwhile a service train to Cowes passes, working wrong-line.

Right: No 29 *Alverstone* heads towards Pier Head from Ryde Esplanade station with an evening train from Ventnor in 1963. The spire of St John's church is prominent on the skyline. The two tracks in the foreground belong to the pier tramway, operated by two Drewry petrol railcars, one of which can just be seen at the Esplanade terminus.

Far left: In the morning sunshine it is possible to get shots of trains coming down the pier from the foreshore. When the author walked to this position the tide appeared to be well out. However, because the foreshore at Ryde is very flat the tide comes in quickly, and within half an hour — by the time this picture was taken of the Shanklin train, headed by No 16 *Ventnor* — he was standing ankle-deep in water.

Left: The line descends sharply to tunnel under the St John's area of Ryde. Here No 27 *Merstone* leaves Ryde Esplanade on the 11.10 to Shanklin during the last summer of steam operation.

Below: No 14 *Fishbourne* emerges from the tunnel to begin the 1-in-66 climb to St John's Road station with a Ventnor-bound train in 1965.

Above: No 33 *Bembridge* departs Ryde St John's Road on its short trip to Esplanade and along the Pier.

Right: No 22 *Brading* arrives at Ryde St John's Road with a train from Cowes in 1965, the last summer of operation. St John's Road was the major base of the island's railway system; out of view to the left of the picture stood Ryde Works, while to the right was the (by 1965) only remaining locomotive depot, in front of which, in the shed yard, can be seen No 24 *Calbourne* (since preserved) and another, unidentified 'O2'. The signal gantry is of particular interest, the two arms with signals attached controlling departure from the two island platform faces onto the down running line of the double-track section to Smallbrook Junction.

RYDE ST. JOHN'S ROAD

Left: This view of Ryde St John's Road shows activity in the spring of 1964, before the summer service had started. A train for Cowes is seen on the left, and one for Ventnor on the right. There are now four arms on the gantry which control access from the two island platforms to either the down or up lines. When the summer service was not in operation the two lines to Smallbrook Junction were operated as two single lines, the down line being for Sandown and Ventnor trains, the up for Cowes trains; this obviated the need to operate Smallbrook Junction 'box but required a smart modification of signal arms at the beginning and end of the summer service. All maintenance of rolling stock was carried out in the works, which can be seen behind the trains, the locomotive shed being immediately to the left of the picture.

Above: Locomotives at rest on Ryde shed towards the end of a summer's day in 1964, including Nos 27 *Merstone*, 31 *Chale* and 33 *Bembridge*.

Left: No 16 *Ventnor* having just taken water prior to its departure from St John's Road for Shanklin in the summer of 1966. Unfortunately it would no longer be able to reach its namesake, the Shanklin–Ventnor section having closed in April of that year.

Above: No 35 *Freshwater* climbing towards Smallbrook Junction on a Ventnor-line train during the summer of 1963, at which time this section was operated as conventional double track.

Left: Isle of Wight 'superpower'! As described in the introduction, the logistics of operating the Summer Saturday service gave rise to two interesting double-headed early-morning workings to move locomotives out to collect stock stored at Sandown and Shanklin. The first was the 07.40 from Ryde Pier Head, which was double-headed from St John's Road to Shanklin. No 35 *Freshwater* pilots No 24 *Calbourne* with a spirited departure from St John's Road in 1965. The second service is illustrated on page 1.

Right: The early-morning mist has just cleared as No 14 *Fishbourne* pilots No 24 *Calbourne* on the 07.40 from Pier Head during the last summer of steam working. In the background can be seen Smallbrook Junction's outer home signal.

Right: A rear view of the above train, with Smallbrook Junction just around the corner.

Left: In the summer of 1963 No 29 *Alverstone* pilots No 17 *Seaview* on the 07.40 approaching Smallbrook Junction, passing under the bridge from which the previous picture was taken.

Below left: On the same day the 07.50 parcels train, headed by Nos 21 *Sandown* and 18 *Ningwood*, passes the outer home signal at Smallbrook Junction.

Right: The straightforward junction layout is clearly seen in this 1965 view of No 27 *Merstone* taking the Ventnor line with an afternoon train, with the Cowes line on the left. Up and down Ventnor-line trains were timed to pass on the double-track section between Smallbrook Junction and Ryde St John's Road, and even a slight delay in the up working would require the down train to be held at the Junction.

Below: Three minutes were allowed for an up train from Shanklin to clear Smallbrook Junction before the 07.40 could enter the single-line section to Brading. However, on this Saturday in 1966 the up train was, for some reason, sufficiently late to allow the author to reach the other side of Smallbrook Junction on foot before the 07.40, headed by Nos 14 and 24, could enter section.

Right: The gentleman seen in the earlier view (page 19) can be seen looking out of the window of the front compartment as the train pulls away from the junction. The knock-on delays of this one incident took some hours to rectify.

Left: The single-line section from Smallbrook Junction to Brading was on a generally falling grade through Whitefield Wood until opening up on the approach to Brading. Here No 29 *Alverstone*, on a Ventnor train, passes the Smallbrook Junction distant in the summer of 1963. On summer Saturdays Ventnor trains were limited-stop, missing out some of the intermediate stations.

Right: Bound for its namesake, No 22 *Brading* passes under the minor road at Truckells Cottages on a summer Saturday in 1965.

Left: No 24 *Calbourne* in a clearing in the woods on a return working to Ryde in the summer of 1965. By this time the locomotive was running in unlined black livery and devoid of nameplates.

Above: No 35 *Freshwater* departs Brading for Ryde in 1966. The location of the signalbox and the track-less outside face of the island platform are a legacy of the branch to Bembridge, closed in 1953.

Left: The Brading signalman prepares to receive the tablet for the single-line section from Smallbrook Junction as No 14 *Fishbourne* arrives with the 11.30 from Ryde to Shanklin in 1966; no tablet was required for the section to Sandown, this being double-track. On the left No 21 *Sandown* awaits the road before continuing its journey to Ryde.

Right: No 24 *Calbourne* waits at Brading with a train from Ventnor in 1963. This would be the last of the island's locomotives to receive an overhaul, running subsequently in unlined black, without nameplates.

South of Brading, the first stretch of the double-track section to Sandown is level and runs briefly alongside the River Yar. The 07.40 from Pier Head is pictured in 1966, No 35 *Freshwater* piloting another, unidentified 'O2'. Rather surprisingly, on such a relatively small island, there are two rivers with the name Yar. That on the west side of the island flows just a short distance, from Freshwater to Yarmouth; here, on the east side, the Yar is a much longer river, flowing from St Catherine's Down, in the south of the island, to Brading Harbour, near Bembridge.

By 1966 closure of the Shanklin–Ventnor section and the Cowes line had reduced the motive-power requirement. This was just as well, for availability of the rapidly wearing-out 'O2s' was itself considerably reduced, necessitating a revision of motive-power diagrams in May. One result was that the 07.50 parcels train was no longer double-headed, as apparent from this view of No 31 *Chale*, recorded at much the same location as the previous photograph.

Left: The retention of double track between Brading and Sandown was essential to maintain timekeeping on a summer Saturday. Trains were booked to pass on this section, and its two-mile length allowed a degree of flexibility in the event of either train's running late. North of Sandown the line rises steeply at 1 in 77 to reach the station; No 29 *Alverstone* is seen at the start of the climb in 1965.

Right: No 21 *Sandown* on the climb to Sandown station in 1964.

In 1964 a passenger service departs Sandown on the double-track section towards Brading as Nos 24 *Calbourne* and 22 *Brading* arrive with the 07.50 parcels train. Loaded to four vehicles, this was unusually long.

Above: A busy scene at Sandown, recorded one Saturday morning in August 1965. No 30 *Shorwell* prepares to depart for Ryde on the 08.40 from Ventnor as the 08.35 from Ryde to Ventnor, formed of set 493, waits to head in the opposite direction, both trains being timed to leave at 09.00. Meanwhile, at the far platform, No 17 *Seaview*, having been uncoupled from the 07.50 vans from Ryde, has been attached to the stock that will form the 09.17 to Ryde.

Right: No 27 *Merstone* pulls away from the outer bay platform of Sandown with the 09.47 to Ryde in 1965. The train will run non-stop to Pier Head.

Above: Sandown station had three platform roads. The outer face of the island platform was used originally for trains to Newport via Alverstone but was retained as a bay platform when that line closed. No 30 *Shorwell* waits to depart for Ventnor in 1965.

Right: Preparing to tackle the 1-in-80 climb to Shanklin, No 26 *Whitwell* makes a spirited departure from Sandown with an afternoon train in 1965. When the line from Sandown to Newport was still in operation the left side of the bracket signal would have supported an arm controlling access to the outer face of the island platform.

Above left: A short, open stretch in the heavily built-up area between Sandown and Shanklin allows a clear view of the 07.40 from Ryde, which is still still double-headed at this location. The locomotives are Nos 21 *Sandown* and 16 *Ventnor*.

Left: By contrast, on the same day in 1965, the 07.50 parcels train, seen earlier (page 33) arriving at Sandown, has now dispensed with the pilot engine and is continuing to Shanklin behind No 22 *Brading* alone.

Above: Between Sandown and Shanklin the land is largely developed. Here No 35 *Freshwater* coasts down the 1-in-80 from Shanklin as it approaches Sandown.

Above: The time is 10.52 as No 18 *Ningwood* arrives at Shanklin with the 10.40 from Ventnor to Ryde. Once this train has cleared the platform (at 10.55) No 14 *Fishbourne* (by now shorn of its nameplates in 1965) will run round its own train, which will then depart as the 11.12 to Ryde.

Right: A mid-afternoon train departs Shanklin for Ventnor behind No 24 *Calbourne* in 1965.

Left: No 20 *Shanklin* approaches the A3020 (Shanklin–Newport) road overbridge as it tackles the 1- in-70 Apse Bank between Shanklin and Wroxall in 1965.

Right: Another photograph of No 20 *Shanklin* between Shanklin and Wroxall, here passing beneath an occupation bridge near Whiteley Bank one Saturday afternoon in the summer of 1965.

Left: No 14 *Fishbourne* leaves Wroxall and begins the descent towards Shanklin with an afternoon train from Ventnor to Ryde one summer Saturday in 1965.

Above: This splendid panorama, recorded from St Boniface Down, features the village of Wroxall and shows clearly the curving approach to the station as a Ventnor-bound train skirts St Martin's Down.

Well caught! The single-line token for the Shanklin–Wroxall section is thrown to the signalman at Wroxall as No 30 *Shorwell* arrives with the 10.10 from Ryde to Ventnor in August 1963. Wroxall station could be said to boast refreshment facilities, as the back door of the village pub (the white rendered building) opened onto the up platform!

No 27 *Merstone* departs Wroxall for Ventnor in 1963. The fireman
had obviously been hard at work while the train was standing at
the platform, preparing for the 1-in-90 climb to the tunnel through
St Boniface Down.

Left: Trains emerge from the tunnel through St Boniface Down directly into Ventnor station, the site for which was excavated from solid rock. Looking for all the world like a model, No 36 *Carisbrooke* makes the point in 1965.

Below left: The same location viewed from a more conventional angle, as No 24 *Calbourne* arrives with a mid-morning train from Ryde in 1965. The signalman has just taken possession of the single-line tablet for the section from Wroxall.

Right: Having run round its train, No 24 *Calbourne* prepares to depart Ventnor on the return journey to Ryde.

No 28 *Ashey* leaves Ventnor with a morning train for Ryde in 1965. The station was nearly 300ft above sea level, enjoying commanding views over the English Channel, but this meant that intending passengers had to carry their luggage up a steep hill from the town. As can be seen, there were two separate platforms, and to reach a train departing from the outer face of the island platform passengers had to use a portable gangway that was used to bridge the gap between the two platforms, there being no passenger access around the buffer-stops.

SMALLBROOK JUNCTION–COWES

No 30 *Shorwell* takes the Cowes line at Smallbrook Junction in the summer of 1963. The Junction signal cabin, which was in the 'V' of the junction, can be seen immediately behind the train. From this point the line (much of which remains open today under the auspices of the Isle of Wight Steam Railway) climbs towards Ashey, on gradients as steep as 1 in 80, then falls towards Havenstreet.

Left: The island's wagons were just as antiquated as the passenger stock. Here, in the summer of 1963, a short goods bound for Newport approaches Havenstreet behind No 21 *Sandown*.

Above: By 1965 the station at Ashey, between Smallbrook and Havenstreet, had been closed and abandoned — hardly surprising, given that the area was (and remains) sparsely populated. Here No 21 *Sandown* passes the derelict building with a train for Cowes.

Left: By 1965 Havenstreet was the only station between Smallbrook and Newport to remain open; it was also the location of a passing-loop on an otherwise single-track line. Here the driver of No 21 *Sandown*, in charge of a train for Ryde, has surrendered the single-line token and is awaiting the passage of a train heading in the opposite direction.

Below left: A few minutes later No 20 *Shanklin* arrives at Havenstreet with the train from Ryde. The signalman is about to hand over the tablet for the section to Newport. Havenstreet is nowadays the headquarters of the Isle of Wight Steam Railway, but although No 24 *Calbourne* has been preserved and runs on the line the sight of two 'O2s' passing cannot be recreated, there being no other survivors.

Right: An interesting juxtaposition of notices at Havenstreet in 1965. On the left is that announcing the closure of the whole of the surviving Isle of Wight system in October 1965 — hardly 'Travelling Made Easier'! In practice the only lines to close would be the line to Cowes and the Shanklin–Ventnor section, and these not until early 1966. Havenstreet station was opened named as Haven Street, but was renamed Havenstreet in accordance with the name of the neighbouring village on 9 June 1958.

Below: The line is still running in an east–west direction as No 29 *Alverstone* passes the derelict station of Whippingham (closed in 1953) on a service to Cowes in 1965.

Left: Just beyond Whippingham the line curved southwest and descended to follow the course of the River Medina upriver towards Newport. No 20 *Shanklin* rounds the curve with a train for Cowes.

Above: Through Newport the line to Cowes made a complete U-turn to cross and skirt the River Medina. Here No 20 *Shanklin* heads southwest close to the river on its way towards the island's capital.

Above: Bound for Ryde, No 27 *Merstone* departs Newport around the U-bend and across the River Medina. On the left of the picture can be seen the brick viaduct which used to carry the branch from Newport to Sandown and Ventnor West. Note also the signal gantry, which at one time controlled access from both lines into Newport station but is by now reduced to a single arm.

Right: No 17 *Seaview* waits to depart from Newport station. The infrastructure reflects the former importance of this centre, which at one time enjoyed rail links to Sandown, Ventnor West and Freshwater and even boasted an engine shed.

Left: As late as 1964 Newport still had a station pilot. Watched intently by a small girl, No 27 *Merstone* attaches a parcels van to the rear of a Ryde-bound train.

Above: No 35 *Freshwater* arrives at Newport with a train from Cowes. The coal wagons would have been loaded at Medina Wharf ready to be hauled to Ryde.

Left: No 31 *Chale* departs Newport with an afternoon train for Cowes

Above: About a mile north of Newport, Mill Pond Viaduct carries the Cowes line across Dodnor Creek, a tributary of the Medina. Here No 24 *Calbourne* crosses the creek with a train for Cowes. Parkhurst Prison is just discernible below the skyline on the right of the picture.

Above: Medina Wharf, about a mile south of Cowes, was the main arrival point for supplies for the railway, notably coal. Each day a locomotive was diagrammed to shunt the wharf before hauling a loaded coal train to Newport and thence to the locomotive shed at Ryde St John's Road. On duty on this occasion, in 1965, was No 27 *Merstone*, seen preparing its train for Newport.

Right: Having completed its shunting duties, *Merstone* leaves the wharf with a lengthy coal train for Newport and Ryde.

Above: A train for Cowes passes the throat of the lines serving Medina Wharf. This view shows the severity of the incline with which loaded coal trains were confronted upon leaving the wharf.

Right: Bound for Newport and Ryde, No 20 *Shanklin* pauses at Mill Hill station, on the southern outskirts of Cowes.

Above: From Mill Hill, half a mile away, the line descends through a tunnel to reach Cowes. Here No 28 *Ashey* arrives at its destination with a train from Ryde.

Right: Having run round its train, *Ashey* waits to depart Cowes on its return journey to Ryde.

THE END

On Sunday 3 October 1965 the LCGB ran a 'Vectis Farewell' trip to mark what was expected, when it was arranged, to be the end of the railways on the island. As it transpired, the Ryde–Shanklin section was reprieved, and closure of Shanklin–Ventnor and the Cowes line delayed until early 1966. After a steam-hauled run on the mainland the LCGB trip toured firstly the Cowes and then the Ventnor line on the island, being seen passing through Ryde Esplanade station behind No 24 *Calbourne* on the outward journey to Cowes.

Calbourne returns to Newport from Cowes with the LCGB trip. A number of photographers had travelled by service trains (which were still in operation) to Newport to get shots of *Calbourne*, but the next service train to Ryde would have missed the LCGB's trip up to Ventnor, so, taking advice from the station staff, a small group of like-minded enthusiasts hired a minibus and driver to give chase to the special.

Above: The first port of call was to photograph the train on its climb up to Sandown. In the meantime, at Ryde St John's Road, *Calbourne* had joined up with No 14 *Fishbourne* for the trip up to Ventnor, as seen here.

Right: Much to the amusement of the driver, everyone piled back into the minibus for a quick dash to the other side of Sandown to record the departure of *Calbourne* and *Fishbourne*.

Above: Yet another dash in the hired minibus permitted a shot of the LCGB special emerging from the tunnel through St Boniface Down into Ventnor station.

Right: The 'gallery' from the LCGB train is set up to photograph No 28 *Ashey* arriving on the following 15.25 service train from Ryde. Having bade farewell to the minibus driver, the author and his fellow enthusiasts caught the 16.30 service train, hauled by *Ashey*, back to Ryde.

Above left: Prior to the laying of the third rail No 24 *Calbourne* hauled one of the 'new' carriages along the line to Shanklin in order to check platform clearances, the formation being seen approaching Sandown in the autumn of 1966.

Left: The same train, by now in atrocious weather conditions, at Brading.

Above: The LCGB ran another trip on the island's one remaining line on 31 December 1966, the last day of steam services. With the third rail already *in situ*, Nos 24 *Calbourne* and 31 *Chale* are seen leaving Ryde St John's Road for Shanklin on the up road, passing a line of the 'new' stock on the erstwhile down line. Both these locomotives would be kept in stock until March 1967 to assist with the conversion work, all others being withdrawn on this day.

DOWN

	am	am	am		am	PM	PM	PM	am	PM	PM	PM	PM	PM	PM	PM	PM	PM	PM
PORTSMOUTH Hbr. } Boat			11 15						11 45									11 45	
RYDE PIER			11 45						12 15		12 45							1 15	
RYDE PIER HEAD	60	11 35	11 42		11 55	12 10	12 20	12 30		12 35	12 42		12 55	1 0	1 10	1 20		1 30	1 35
Esplanade		11a39	11a47			12a25	12a39	12a47		12a39	12a47					1a25			1c39
St. John's Road		11a43	11a51			12a29	12a43	12a51		12a43	12a51			1 5		1a29		1 35	1a43
Smallbrook Jn.		11 46	11 54			12 32				12 46	12 54								1 46
Brading	arr				12 7	12 21	12 37				12 59		1 7		1 21	1 37			
	dep		11 59		12 10	12 22	12 39			12 59			1 10		1 22	1 39			
Sandown	arr		12 3		12 14		12 43						1 14			1 43			
	dep		12 5							1 5				1 26		1 48			
Shanklin	arr		12a10			12a31	12 48			1X10			1 16	1X31		1 53			
	dep		12 16			12 36				1 16			1 36						
Wroxall	arr		12X24			12X44				1X24			1X44						
	dep		12 24			12 47				1 27			1 47						
VENTNOR	arr		12 32			12 52				1 32			1 52						
Ashey	arr							12 50									1 50		
Havenstreet	dep	11X54							12X54								1X54		2 3½
NEWPORT	arr	12 3½							1 3½								2 3½		2 7
Medina Wharf	dep	12 7							1 7								2 7		
Gas Works Siding		R							R								R		
Mill Hill		12 16							1 16								2 16		
COWES	arr	12 18							1 18								2 18		

UP

	am	am	am	PM	am	PM	PM	PM	PM	PM	PM	PM	PM	Freight	PM	PM	PM	PM
COWES	dep			11 28							12 28			12 40				
Mill Hill				11 30½							12 30½							
Gas Works Siding													12 45					
Medina Wharf													12 45					
NEWPORT	arr			11 39							12 39	12 57						
Havenstreet	arr										12X52						1 20	
	dep			11 55							12 55						1 30	
Ashey				12 0							1 0							
VENTNOR	dep	11 20			11 40					12 20			12 40					
Wroxall	arr	11X25			11X45					12X25			12X45					
	dep	11 26			11 46					12 26			12 46					
Shanklin	arr	11X32			11X52					12X32			12X52					
	dep	11 35			11 55	12 12				12 35			12 55		1 12			
Sandown	arr	11 39			11 59		12 16		12 31	12 39			12 59					
	dep	11 31	11 42		12 1		12 16		12 31	12 42			1 1		1 16		1 31	
Brading	arr	11 35			12 5		12 20		12 35				1 5		1 20		1 35	
	dep	11 39			12 8		12 23		12 39			1 8			1 23		1 39	
Smallbrook Jn.		11 44	11 50½	12 4	12 13		12 28		12 44	12 50½		1 13			1 28		1 44	
RYDE St. John's Road	arr	11b54	12a 7	12a16	12 23		12 35		12b54	1 0	1a 7	1a16	1 23		1 28		1 40	
Esplanade		11c59	12a11	12a21					12c59		1a11	1c21						
PIER HEAD	arr	11 50	12 1	12 12	12 23	12 28	12 35	12 40		12 50	1 1	1 5	1 13		1 23	1 28	1 35	1 50
RYDE PIER } Boat				12 20			12 50			1 20			1 50				1 50	
PORTSMOUTH Hbr.	24			12 50					1 20			1 50					2 20	

Above: Copy of parts of pages from the BR working timetable for summer 1963.

Left: By the time the LCGB special returned from Shanklin the earlier gloomy conditions had given way to bright sunshine, as apparent from this photograph of the train north of Brading.

Right: Diagram illustrating the pathways and passing places (taken from the tables above) over a one-hour cycle. The coloured lines show the passage of the train, identified in the key, between each location on the vertical grid. The continuous lines representing trains from Ryde, and the broken lines those to Ryde. Station stopping time is indicated by the vertical part of the coloured lines, and shows the very limited time for delay. Trains crossing between Ryde Esplanade and Smallbrook, and between Brading and Sandown show the advantage of the double track in these sections.

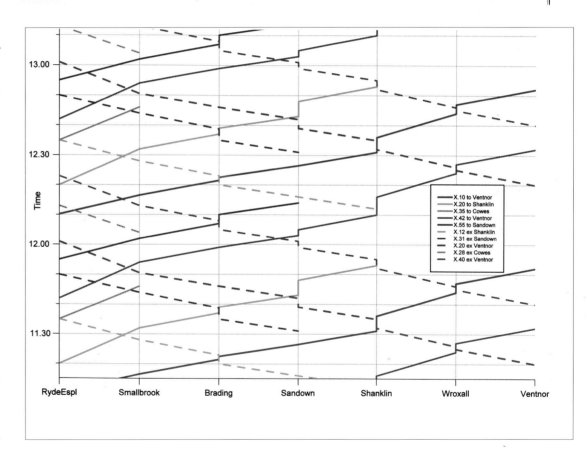

X.10 to Ventnor	
X.20 to Shanklin	
X.35 to Cowes	
X.42 to Ventnor	
X.55 to Sandown	
X.12 ex Shanklin	
X.31 ex Sandown	
X.20 ex Ventnor	
X.28 ex Cowes	
X.40 ex Ventnor	

Sunset of steam. An unidentified 'O2' hauls a Ryde-bound train
near Brading as the sun sets on the last day of steam-operated
passenger trains.